XTREME HORROR LAB

THE SCIENCE OF PSYCHIC POWERS

A&D Xtreme
An imprint of Abdo Publishing
abdobooks.com

RUBY DANIELS

TAKE IT TO THE XTREME!

GET READY FOR AN EXTREME ADVENTURE! THE PAGES OF THIS BOOK WILL TAKE YOU INTO THE SPOOKY WORLD OF UNEXPLAINED PHENOMENA. WHEN YOU HAVE FINISHED READING THIS BOOK, TAKE THE XTREME CHALLENGE ON PAGE 43 ABOUT WHAT YOU'VE LEARNED!

ABDOBOOKS.COM
Published by Abdo Publishing, a division of ABDO, PO Box 398166, Minneapolis, Minnesota 55439.

Printed in the United States of America, North Mankato, MN.
052024
092024

THIS BOOK CONTAINS RECYCLED MATERIALS

Design: Kelly Doudna, Mighty Media, Inc.
Production: Mighty Media, Inc.
Editor: Jessica Rusick
Cover Photograph: Indre/Adobe Stock
Interior Photographs: Aida Servi/Shutterstock Images, pp. 26-27; DedMityay/Adobe Stock, pp. 4-5; elena_suvorova/Adobe Stock, pp. 12-13; Everett Collection/Shutterstock Images, pp. 32-33; fran_kie/Shutterstock Images, pp. 30-31; Francis Wickware/Wikimedia Commons, p. 27; Ground Picture/Shutterstock Images, pp. 40-41; happy_author/Adobe Stock, p. 45; Harry Wedzinga/Adobe Stock, p. 44 (top); Indre/Adobe Stock, p. 1; Joaquin Ossorio Castillo/Shutterstock Images, pp. 14-15; JOSEPH PREZIOSO/Getty Images, pp. 38-39; Kathy Hutchins/Shutterstock Images, pp. 24-25; Kiselev Andrey Valerevich/Shutterstock Images, pp. 8-9; Library of Congress, pp. 13, 16-17, 18, 19 (inset); LIONEL CIRONNEAU/AP Images, pp. 6-7; NASA/JPL-Caltech/MSSS/Wikimedia Commons, pp. 22-23; New Africa/Shutterstock Images, pp. 10-11; Petr Smagin/Shutterstock Images, pp. 20-21; RomixImage/Adobe Stock, p. 19 (background); Scott a hurst/Wikimedia Commons, pp. 34-35; StepPro/Adobe Stock, p. 44 (bottom); sun ok/Shutterstock Images, p. 42; The Print Collector/Alamy Photo, pp. 36-37; Thomson Jay Hudson/Wikimedia Commons, p. 20; US Army Office of Public Affairs/Wikimedia Commons, p. 30; YAKOBCHUK VIACHESLAV/Shutterstock Images, pp. 28-29
Design Elements: Dominik Hladik/Shutterstock Images (moon); nikiteev_konstantin/Shutterstock Images (curves); pixelparticle/Shutterstock Images (stars); pixssa/Shutterstock Images (stretchy circle)

LIBRARY OF CONGRESS CONTROL NUMBER: 2023949613

PUBLISHER'S CATALOGING-IN-PUBLICATION DATA
Names: Daniels, Ruby, author.
Title: The science of psychic powers / by Ruby Daniels
Description: Minneapolis, Minnesota : Abdo Publishing, 2025 | Series: Xtreme horror lab | Includes online resources and index.
Identifiers: ISBN 9781098293215 (lib. bdg.) | ISBN 9798384912484 (ebook)
Subjects: LCSH: Psychic ability--Juvenile literature. | Parapsychology--Juvenile literature. | Extrasensory perception--Juvenile literature. | Science--Juvenile literature.
Classification: DDC 133.82--dc23

TABLE OF CONTENTS

CHAPTER 1

FUTURE SIGHT?

Some psychics, known as palmists, practice palmistry or palm reading. Palmists predict someone's future based on the features of the person's palms.

Strange things keep happening to you. You had a dream about your old teacher. Then you saw him at the store the next day! You somehow knew there would be a pop quiz before it happened. You even guessed a coin toss seven times in a row! It's like you can see the future. Could your psychic powers be real?

CHAPTER 2
TERRIFYING TERMINOLOGY

Israeli psychic Uri Geller claimed he could bend metal objects with his mind. But scientists say Geller's feats were illusions.

There are two main categories of psychic powers. One is psychokinesis, also known as telekinesis. This is the ability to move things with the mind. People with psychokinesis can move people and objects without touching them.

The second type of psychic power is extrasensory perception (ESP). People with ESP may communicate through thoughts or read minds. They may see the future. Or they may be able to sense **supernatural** beings, such as ghosts.

ESP is sometimes called a "sixth sense." That's because it involves knowledge beyond the five senses.

CHAPTER 3

GAZING INTO THE PAST

Psychic powers have been part of human culture since ancient times. Ancient psychics had many names. They were called seers, oracles, shamans, and more. Ancient psychics claimed to interpret **supernatural** signs. This process is called divination. Psychics used signs to predict the future and explain current events.

One divination method is crystal gazing. Psychics look into crystal balls and try to see future events.

Psychics were respected in ancient societies. Everyday people went to them for advice. Psychics' predictions helped people decide how to solve problems. Psychics could also explain why bad things, such as illness, happened. At the time, science had not advanced enough to correctly explain these things.

The Tholos of Delphi in Greece was built between 380 and 360 BCE. Citizens and government leaders visited the site before making important decisions.

The Oracle of Delphi (*left*) was an ancient group of Greek priestesses. They claimed to channel the god Apollo to predict the future.

XTREME FACT

Ancient rulers often consulted seers for advice on when to wage war. So, many seers had great political and military power.

CHAPTER 4

CHANGING TIMES

Religions, such as Christianity, gained popularity in the **Middle Ages**. Christianity officially banned divination. Psychic powers became associated with evil. As Christianity's influence grew, fewer people went to psychics.

Nostradamus was a famous seer in the 1500s. He published a book of prophecies based on his visions of the future.

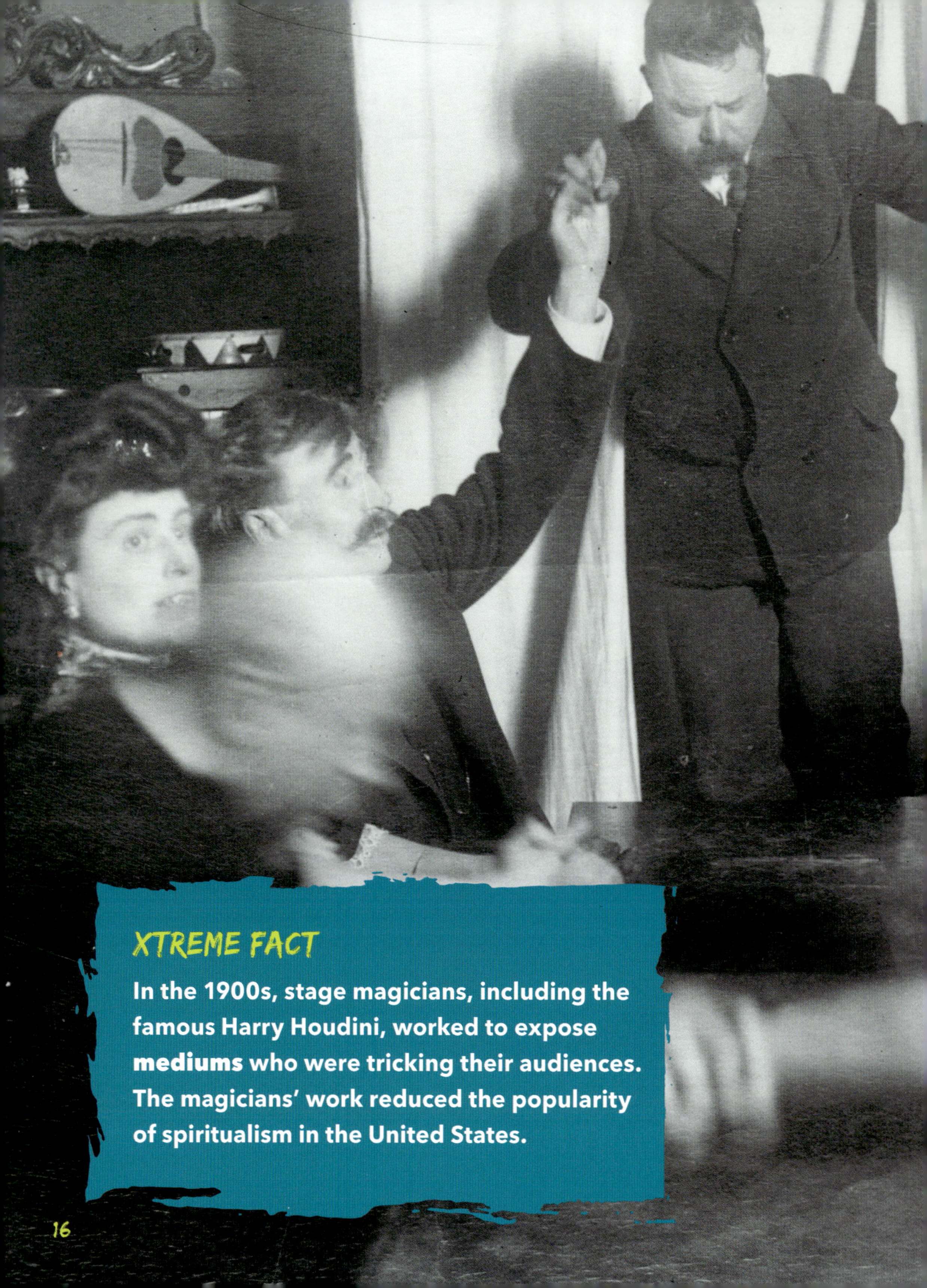

XTREME FACT

In the 1900s, stage magicians, including the famous Harry Houdini, worked to expose **mediums** who were tricking their audiences. The magicians' work reduced the popularity of spiritualism in the United States.

In the mid-1800s, a movement called spiritualism gained popularity. People called spirit **mediums** claimed they could psychically communicate with the dead. The mediums offered their services for money. They gained many followers. But churches continued to call these activities evil.

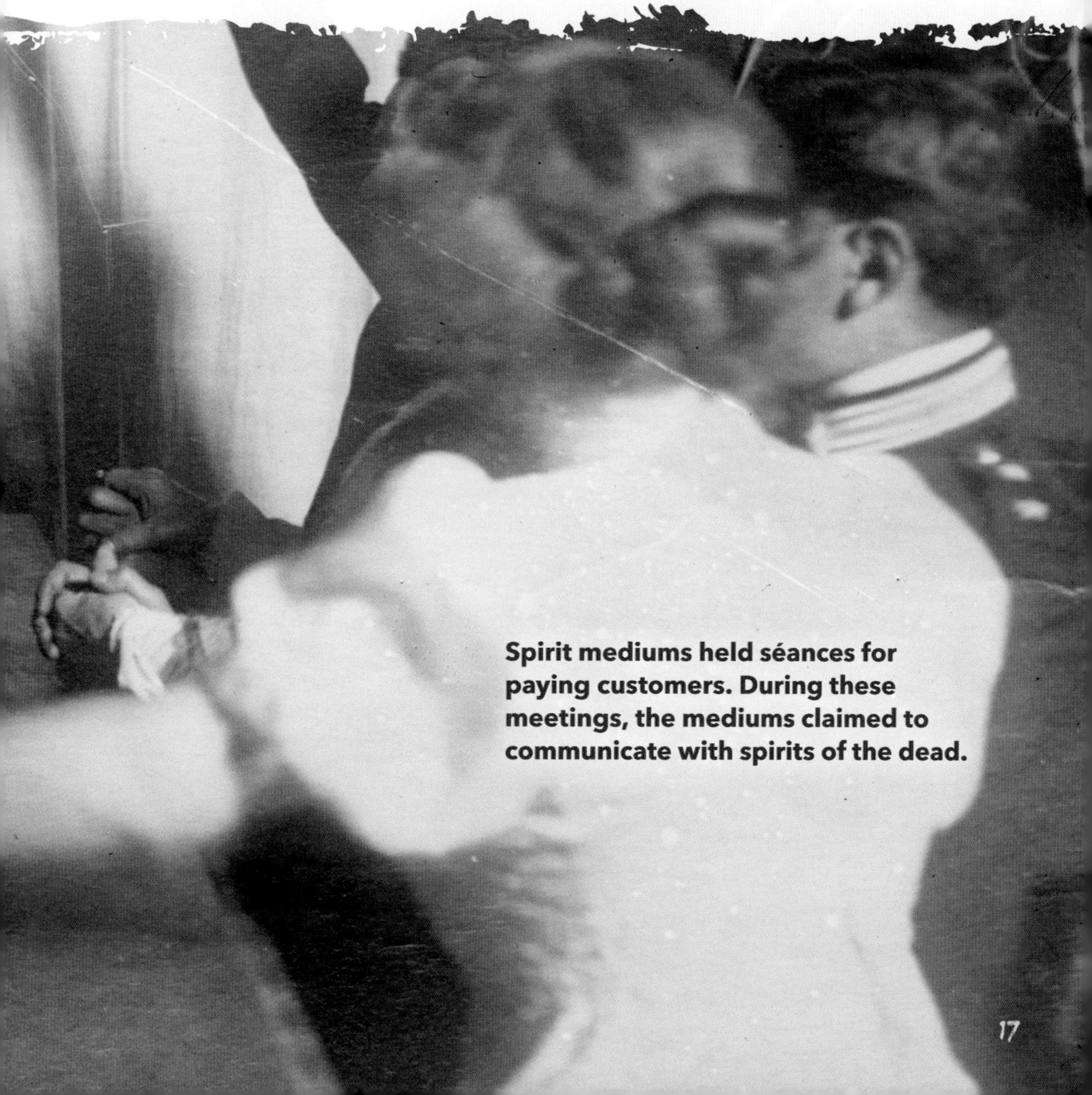

Spirit mediums held séances for paying customers. During these meetings, the mediums claimed to communicate with spirits of the dead.

Spiritualism became popular for several reasons. During the mid-1800s, many people died during the **American Civil War**. In the early 1900s, many people died during **World War I**. Following these wars, grieving people wanted to connect with dead loved ones.

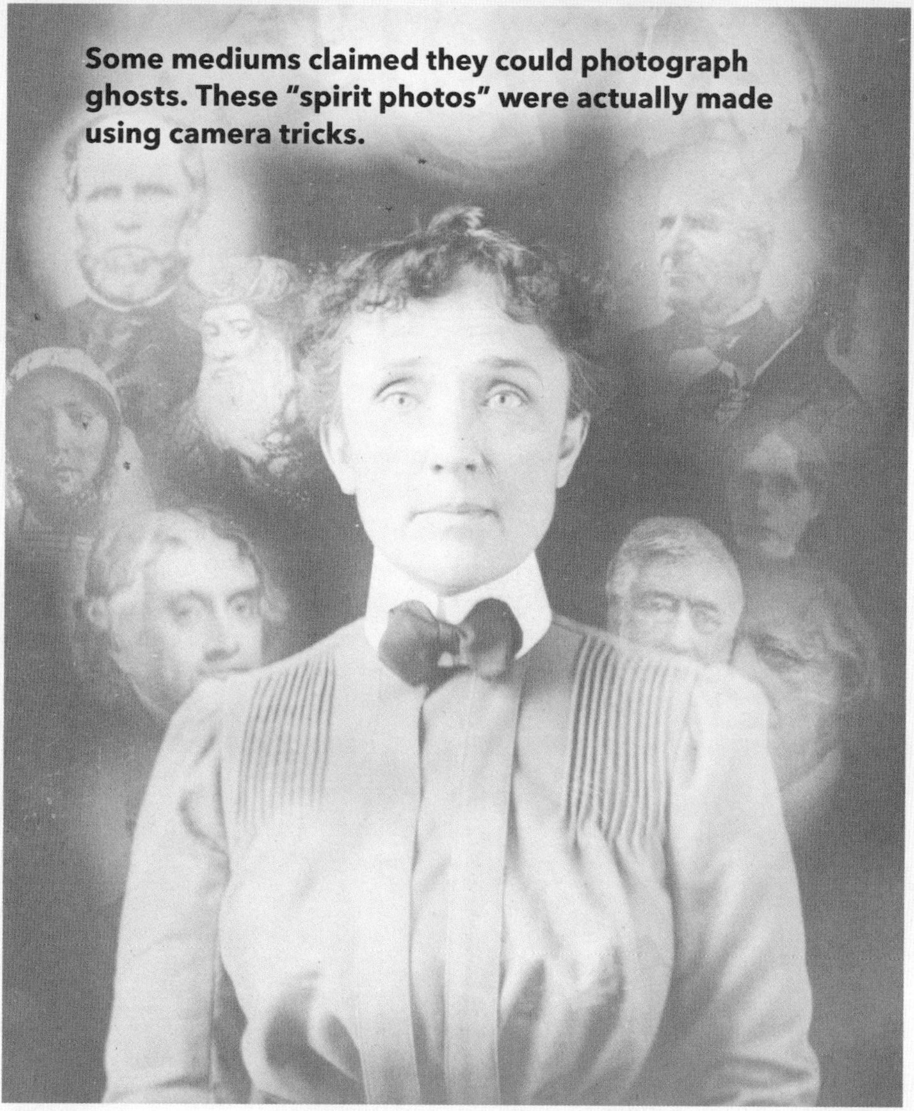

Some mediums claimed they could photograph ghosts. These "spirit photos" were actually made using camera tricks.

CHAPTER 5

INVESTIGATIONS BEGIN

The Society for Psychical Research investigated many psychics, including Leonora Piper (*inset*). Some society members concluded Piper was a fraud. But others believed her powers were real.

As the spiritualism movement grew, scientists began to research psychic performers. They founded organizations to investigate claims of ESP. The researchers used scientific methods to search for proof of psychic powers. They discovered many psychics were frauds. But they could not disprove all psychic claims.

XTREME FACT

Early research on psychic powers developed into the field of parapsychology. This is the study of psychic powers and other paranormal happenings. Today, some universities have parapsychology departments.

During the **Cold War**, the **Central Intelligence Agency (CIA)** studied psychic powers for military purposes. The CIA mostly tested whether subjects could remotely view places, people, and objects using only the mind. Remote viewing power would help the CIA spy on targets. But the CIA's remote viewing studies were **inconclusive**.

Remote viewers are meant to give specific information about a faraway location, person, or object. During some CIA tests, remote viewers were asked to target the surface of Mars (*pictured*)!

CHAPTER 6

PSYCHICS & SCIENCE TODAY

Belief in psychic powers continues in modern times. In a 2017 YouGov poll, 34 percent of Americans said they've had a psychic episode, such as predicting the future. Some modern psychics have popular stage and television shows. They perform psychic acts for large audiences.

XTREME FACT

Police officers and detectives occasionally employ psychics to help solve crimes.

Tyler Henry is a famous modern psychic who claims to speak with the dead. He has a TV show and tours the world.

Researchers use several tests to check for psychic powers. The tests determine whether subjects can predict something more frequently than is likely by chance. One test involves a deck of 25 cards called Zener cards. Each Zener card has one of five symbols. Test subjects are asked to use ESP to name the order of the symbols in a shuffled deck.

XTREME FACT

In the 1930s, one man supposedly guessed all 25 Zener cards in a row. The odds of doing this by chance are 1 in 300 quadrillion.

Zener cards debuted in the 1930s. Early tests were criticized by scientists. There were different ways subjects could cheat. One was by seeing through the thin cards.

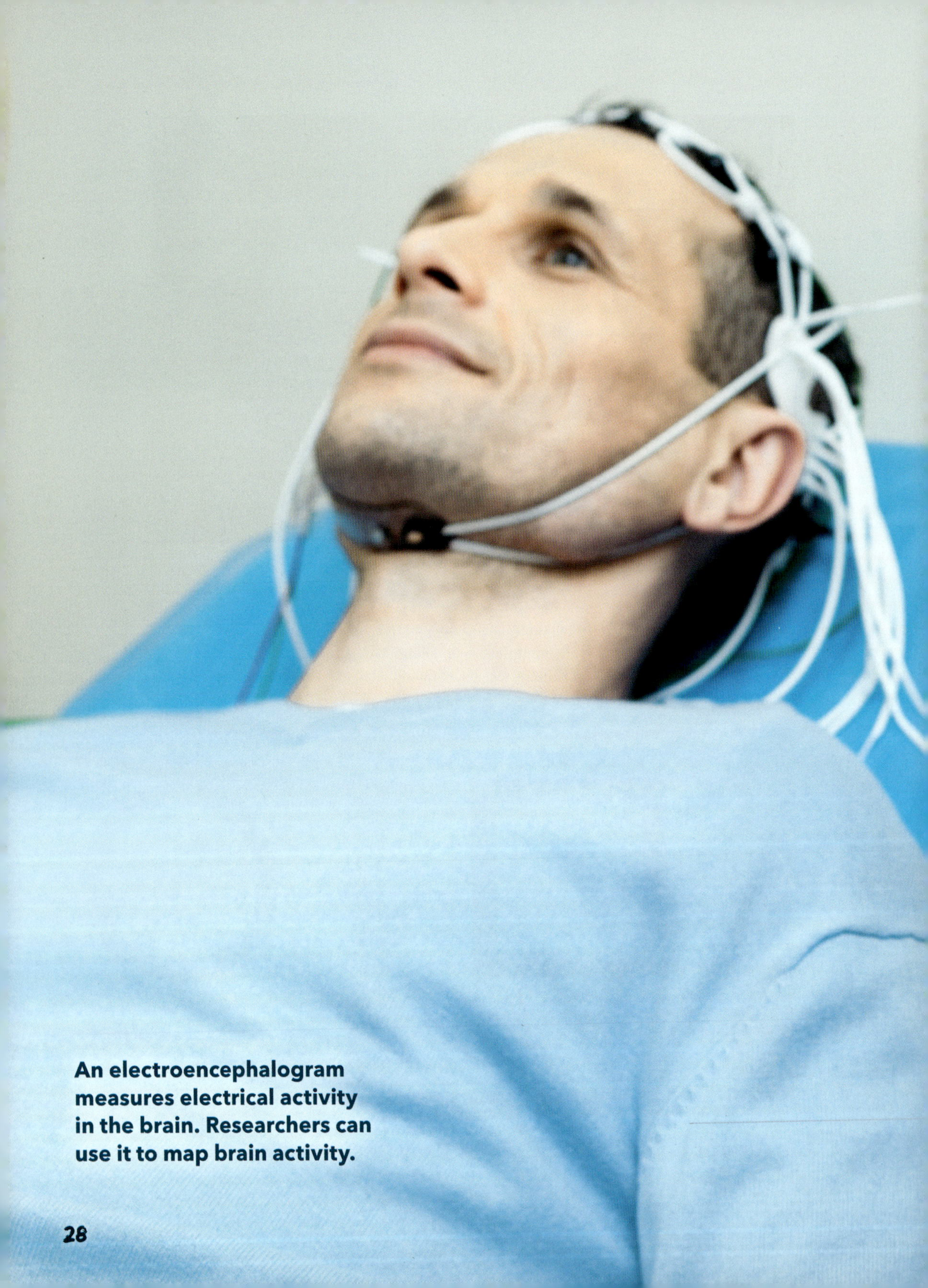

An electroencephalogram measures electrical activity in the brain. Researchers can use it to map brain activity.

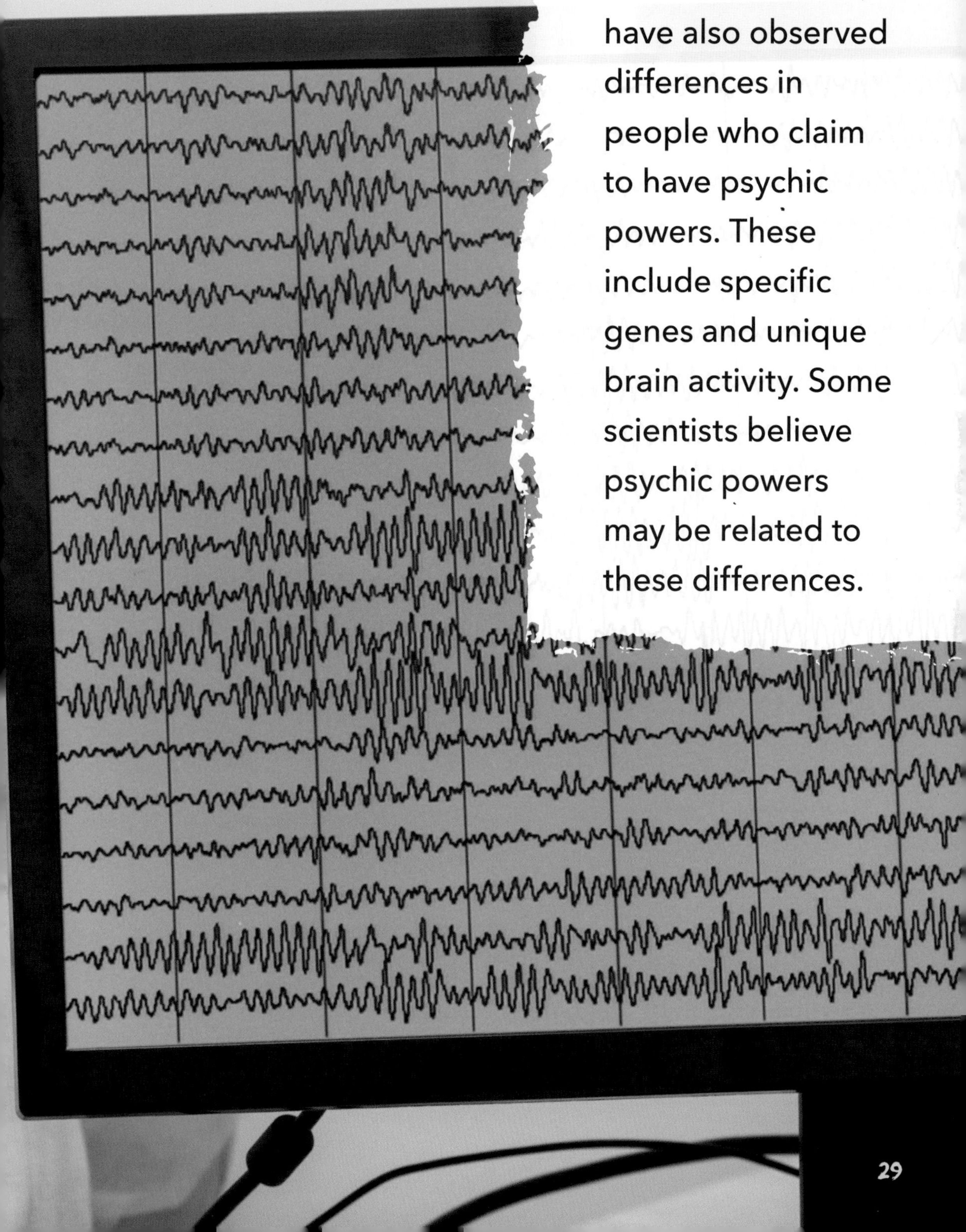

Researchers have also observed differences in people who claim to have psychic powers. These include specific genes and unique brain activity. Some scientists believe psychic powers may be related to these differences.

CHAPTER 7

STUDIES & SECOND GUESSES

Some studies have found additional evidence of psychic powers. In the 1990s, two researchers reviewed old **CIA** remote viewing studies. One researcher believed the studies produced evidence of psychic abilities. In 2023, another study claimed to find evidence of remote viewing abilities. However, experts disagree on whether these studies prove psychic powers exist.

Major General Albert Stubblebine (*inset*) championed the US government's research into psychic powers. He believed psychic powers would allow soldiers to turn invisible and walk through walls.

PHREN
Come In
and have
Your Head
Read
YOUR H
IS LIK
OPEN
To U

Research that finds evidence of psychic powers may seem persuasive. But studies must be repeated many times by different scientists to be considered strong evidence. The studies must achieve similar results. Researchers often have trouble repeating psychic studies. This suggests there were problems with the originals.

Many scientists call psychic ability pseudoscience because it has no scientific basis. Another example of pseudoscience is phrenology. This is the belief that someone's head shape determines their personality.

CHAPTER 8

SHADOWS OF DOUBT

In 2009, psychic Connie Sonne (*left*) attempted to win $1 million by demonstrating her powers. But she was unable to correctly identify cards in a sealed envelope.

There are other reasons people doubt psychic powers exist. Organizations have offered money to anyone who can prove they have psychic powers. But no one has won the money. **Skeptics** point out that psychics could likely use their powers to stop tragedies. But tragedies still happen. So, it's unlikely that people have psychic powers.

There are many ways people can fake having psychic powers. A pretend psychic may predict someone's future by saying things that could apply to many people. Pretend psychics may also research people before mind readings. The psychics then use the researched information during the readings.

XTREME FACT

True psychic powers haven't been proven to exist. But future brain technology may be able to mimic telepathy.

Some psychics claim to read minds but really read muscles. People make tiny, involuntary movements that can reveal their thoughts or feelings. Psychics look for these movements and use them to interpret someone's thoughts.

CHAPTER 9

WHY DO PEOPLE BELIEVE?

People believe in psychic powers for many reasons. Sometimes, people struggle to accept that tragic or random events can happen. They feel a need to find meaning behind these events. This leads them to believe **supernatural** explanations without investigating further.

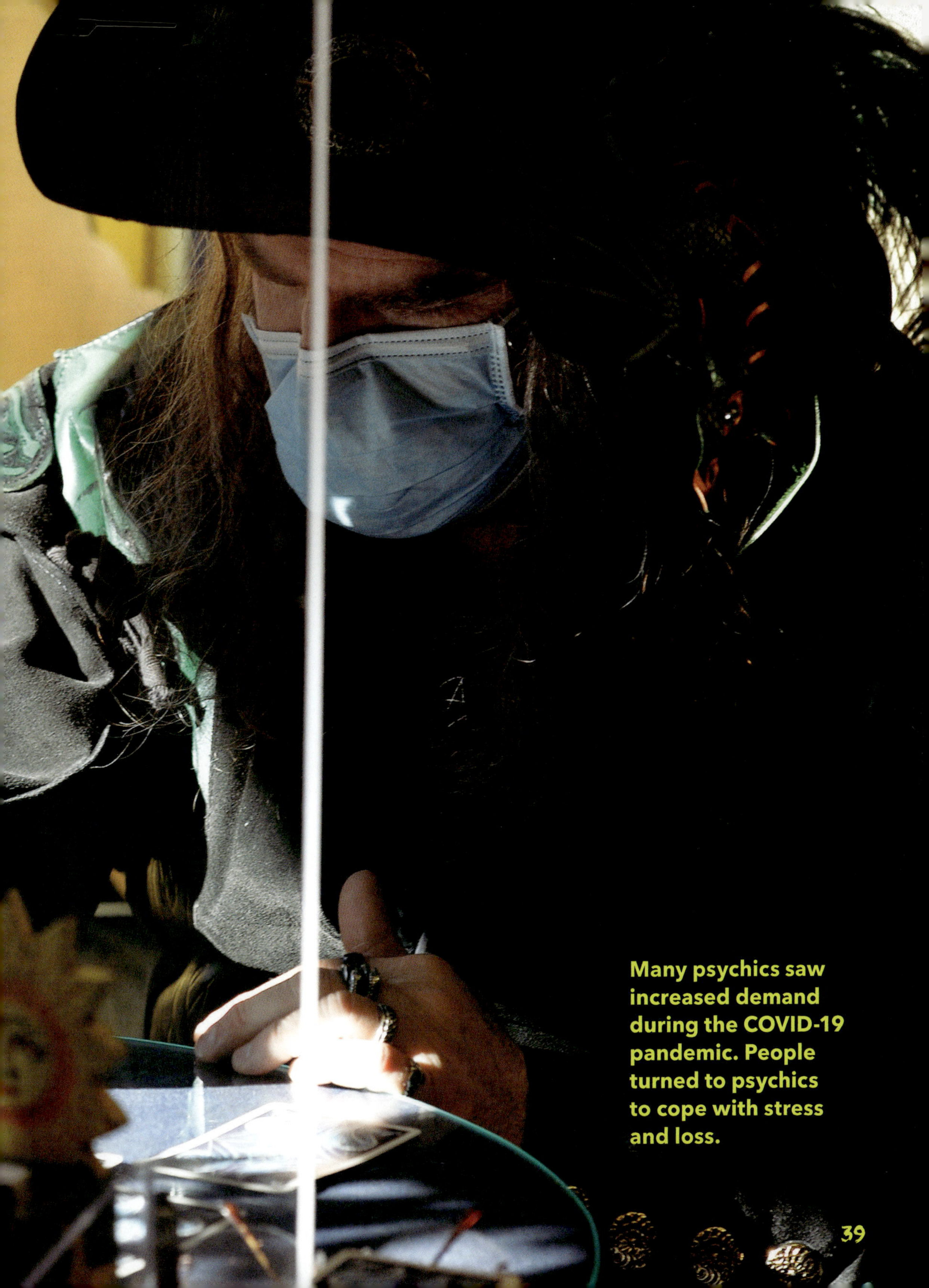

Many psychics saw increased demand during the COVID-19 pandemic. People turned to psychics to cope with stress and loss.

People may also mistake mental illness for psychic powers. Some mental illnesses such as **schizophrenia** can cause **hallucinations**. People who experience hallucinations sense things that aren't there. So, they may incorrectly believe they have psychic powers.

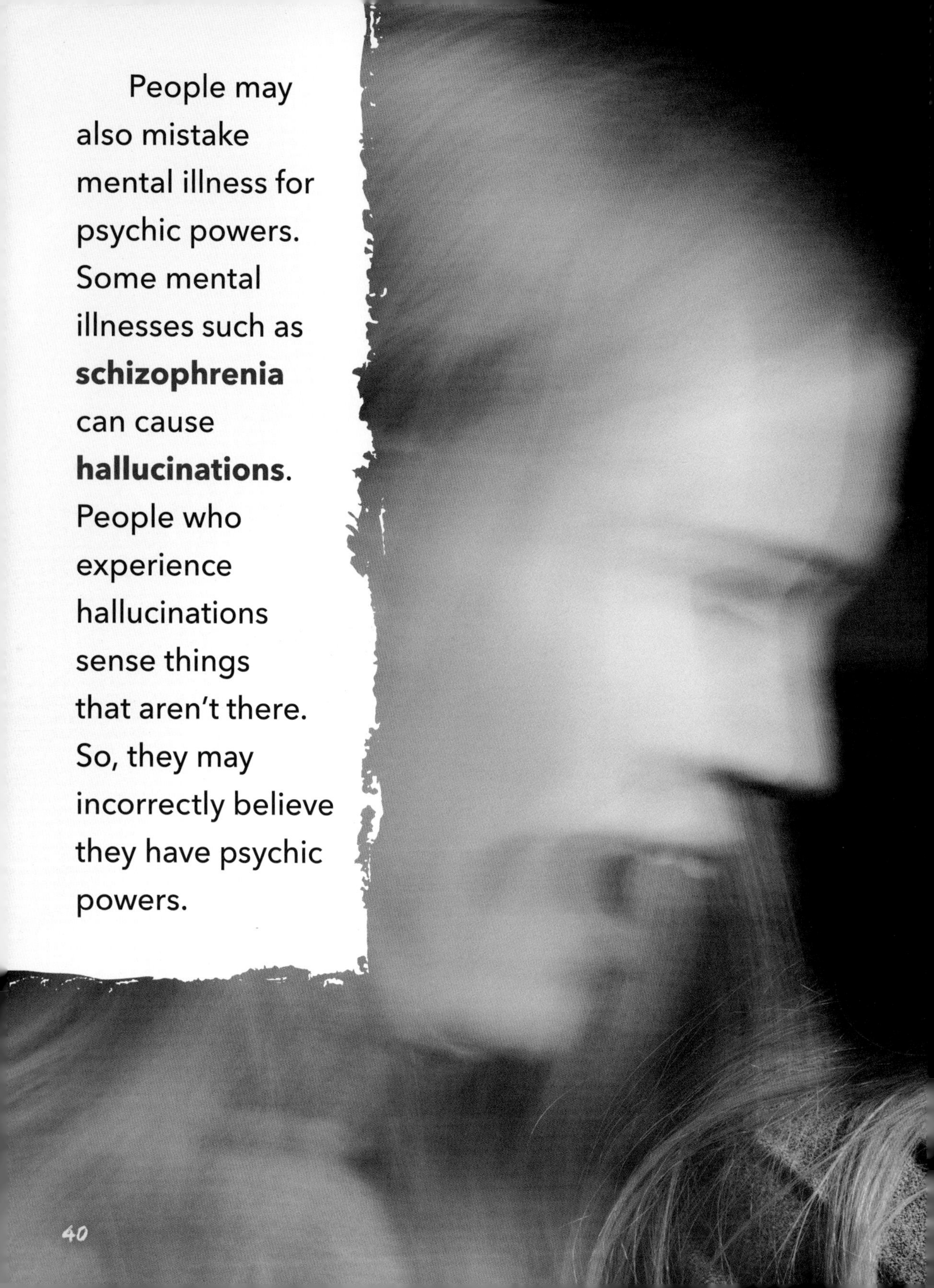

Hallucinations can involve any of the five senses. The most common hallucination is hearing voices.

CHAPTER 10

COULD PSYCHIC POWERS EXIST?

People have believed in psychic powers since ancient times. But scientists have been unable to prove that psychic powers exist. In the future, new studies may uncover more about psychics. Until then, people should approach evidence of psychic powers with curious but **skeptical** minds.

XTREME CHALLENGE

TAKE THE QUIZ BELOW AND PUT WHAT YOU'VE LEARNED TO THE TEST!

1) What are the two main types of psychic powers?

2) After reading this book, do you believe that people can have psychic powers?

3) Why do you think people have believed in psychic powers for so long?

4) How are Zener cards used to test people for psychic abilities?

5) Why is it important to question people who claim to be psychics?

PSYCHIC POWERS HORROR LAB

Use a die to test your family and friends for psychic powers!

WHAT YOU NEED

- partner
- 1 six-sided die
- paper
- pen or pencil

WHAT YOU DO

1. First, test for ESP. Ask your partner to write down the number they think will come up on the die.

2. Roll the die. Record whether your partner's guess was right or wrong.

3. Repeat the test nine more times.

4 Next, test for psychokinesis. Say aloud a number on the die. Ask your partner to move the die with their mind as it rolls so that it lands on that number.

5 Roll the die. Record whether the die landed on the chosen number.

6 Repeat the test nine more times.

CONSIDER THIS

There is a 1 in 6, or about 17 percent, chance that a die will land on a given number. This means your partner will likely pass the tests 17 percent of the time by chance alone. (That's roughly 2 out of 10 rolls.) Passing 3 times would be slightly less likely by chance alone, and so on. There is a 1 in 66 million chance that your partner would pass all 10 rolls. How many times did your partner succeed? If it was more than 17 percent of the time, why might that be?

GLOSSARY

American Civil War—the war between the Northern and Southern states from 1861 to 1865.

Central Intelligence Agency (CIA)—a US government agency that gathers information about foreign nations to help protect US national security.

Cold War—a period of tension and hostility between the United States and its allies and the Soviet Union and its allies after World War II.

hallucination—an experience of having heard, seen, smelled, or tasted something that seemed real but was not actually real.

inconclusive—reaching no conclusion.

medium—a person who claims to communicate with spirits.

Middle Ages—a period in European history that lasted from about 500 CE to about 1500 CE.

schizophrenia—a mental illness in which a person does not know what sights, sounds, and experiences are real or what they are imagining.

skeptic—one who has an attitude of doubt or disbelief. Someone who has this attitude is skeptical.

supernatural—relating to magic, spirits, or other things that cannot be explained by science or nature.

World War I—from 1914 to 1918, fought in Europe. Great Britain, France, Russia, the United States, and their allies were on one side. Germany, Austria-Hungary, and their allies were on the other side.

ONLINE RESOURCES

Booklinks
NONFICTION NETWORK
FREE! ONLINE NONFICTION RESOURCES

To learn more about psychic powers, please visit **abdobooklinks.com** or scan this QR code. These links are routinely monitored and updated to provide the most current information available.

INDEX